Home Maintenance Log For:

Address:_____

_____

Date of Purchase:_____

Systems Maintenance By Month

JANUARY

Clean Pipes (Descale overnight)
Clean Showerheads and Taps
Clean and Recaulk Shower/Sinks
Clear Ice Dams In Gutters

FEBRUARY

Deep Clean Oven and Stovetop
Clean Washer
Clean Dyer and Check Vent
Clean Dishwasher & Check Filter

MARCH

Deep Spring Clean
Check Roof for Soft Spots
Check Sump Pump
Clean Gutters

Systems Maintenance By Month

APRIL
Spring Clean Kitchen
Vacuum HVAC Unit
Inspect Attic
Have AC Tuned

MAY
Check Exhaust Fans
Check Ceiling Fan Blades/Dust
Check Weather Stripping
Fix Rust Spots

JUNE
Clean Window Wells
Remove Dead Limbs From Trees
Touchup Paint
Remove Dead Plants From Flowerbeds

Systems Maintenance By Month

JULY

- Clean/Stain Deck
- Maintain Garage Door
- Power Wash Concrete
- Check Ductwork for Leaks

AUGUST

- Clean Garbage Disposal
- Clean Out Freezer
- Clean Window Treatments
- Change Air Filters

SEPTEMBER

- Flush Water Heater
- Furnace Tune-Up
- Check Pantry for Expired Food
- Check Carbon Monoxide Detectors

Systems Maintenance By Month

OCTOBER

- Remove Exterior Hoses & Drain
- Vacuum & Clean Furnace
- Deep Clean Microwave
- Winterize AC

NOVEMBER

- Vacuum Fridge Coils
- Deep Clean Fridge
- Clean Fridge Drain Pan
- Clean Circuit Breakers

DECEMBER

- Test Electrical Outlets
- Run Water in Unused Rooms
- Inspect Fire Extinguishers
- Replace Smoke Detector Batteries

Repairman Contact Information

Company Name:_____
Phone Number:_____
Email:_____
Technician Name:_____

Company Name:_____
Phone Number:_____
Email:_____
Technician Name:_____

Company Name:_____
Phone Number:_____
Email:_____
Technician Name:_____

Company Name:_____
Phone Number:_____
Email:_____
Technician Name:_____

Repairman Contact Information

Company Name:_____
Phone Number:_____
Email:_____
Technician Name:_____

Company Name:_____
Phone Number:_____
Email:_____
Technician Name:_____

Company Name:_____
Phone Number:_____
Email:_____
Technician Name:_____

Company Name:_____
Phone Number:_____
Email:_____
Technician Name:_____

Repairman Contact Information

Company Name:_____
Phone Number:_____
Email:_____
Technician Name:_____

Company Name:_____
Phone Number:_____
Email:_____
Technician Name:_____

Company Name:_____
Phone Number:_____
Email:_____
Technician Name:_____

Company Name:_____
Phone Number:_____
Email:_____
Technician Name:_____

Home Warranty Information:

Company:_____

Premium Paid:_____

Contract Length:_____

Policy Number:_____

Customer Service Number:_____

Online Login User Name:_____

Online Login Password:_____

Appliances Covered:

Refrigerator	Ice Maker
Stove	Garbage Disposal
Washer	Other
Dryer	Other
Dishwasher	Other
Built-In Microwave	Other
Trash Compactor	Other

Home Warranty Information (Continued):

Systems Covered:

	Air Conditioning
	Heating
	Electrical
	Door Bell
	Smoke Detectors
	Ceiling Fans
	Water Heater

	Central Vac.
	Septic Pump
	Well Pump
	Other
	Other
	Other
	Other

Usage Log:

Date	What Was Serviced	Problem	Service Technician

Home Warranty Information (Continued):

Date	What Was Serviced	Problem	Service Technician

Appliance Information

Date of Purchase	Appliance	Purchased From	Price	Serial Number	Warranty

Appliance Information

Date of Purchase	Appliance	Purchased From	Price	Serial Number	Warranty

Appliance Information

Date of Purchase	Appliance	Purchased From	Price	Serial Number	Warranty

Appliance Repair Log

Date of Service	Appliance	Repairman	Contact Info	Cost	Warranty

Appliance Repair Log

Date of Service	Appliance	Repairman	Contact Info	Cost	Warranty

Appliance Repair Log

Date of Service	Appliance	Repairman	Contact Info	Cost	Warranty

Monthly Maintenance Log

Date	Check Smoke Detectors	Change Furnace Filter	Other:	Other:	Performed By (Initials)

Monthly Maintenance Log

Date	Check Smoke Detectors	Change Furnace Filter	Other:	Other:	Performed By (Initials)

Monthly Maintenance Log

Date	Check Smoke Detectors	Change Furnace Filter	Other:	Other:	Performed By (Initials)

Quarterly Maintenance Log

Date	Check Basement/Crawl Space For Leaks	Clean Fridge	Clean Baseboards	Check Shower/Sink Drain Issues	Performed By (Initials)

Quarterly Maintenance Log

Date	Check Basement/Crawl Space For Leaks	Clean Fridge	Clean Baseboards	Check Shower/Sink Drain Issues	Performed By (Initials)

Quarterly Maintenance Log

Date	Check Basement/Crawl Space For Leaks	Clean Fridge	Clean Baseboards	Check Shower/Sink Drain Issues	Performed By (Initials)

Yearly Maintenance Log

Date	Smoke Detector Batteries	Carbon Monoxide Detector	Clean Gutters	Other:	Other:	Performed By (Initials)

Yearly Maintenance Log

Date	Smoke Detector Batteries	Carbon Monoxide Detector	Clean Gutters	Other:	Other:	Performed By (Initials)

Yearly Maintenance Log

Date	Smoke Detector Batteries	Carbon Monoxide Detector	Clean Gutters	Other:	Other:	Performed By (Initials)

Notes

Notes

Notes

Notes

Notes

Notes

Notes

Notes

Notes

Notes

Notes

Notes

Notes

Notes

Notes

Notes

Notes

Notes

Notes

Notes

Notes

Notes

Notes

Notes

Notes

Notes

Notes

Notes

Notes

Notes

Notes

Notes

Notes

Notes

Notes

Notes

Notes

Notes

Notes

Notes

Notes

Notes

Notes

Notes

Notes

Notes

Notes

Notes

Notes

Notes

Notes

Notes

Notes

Notes

Notes

Notes

Notes

Notes

Notes

Notes

Notes

Notes

Notes

Notes

Notes

Notes

Notes

Notes

Notes

Notes

Notes

Notes

Notes

Notes

Notes

Notes

Notes

Notes

Notes

Notes

Notes

Notes

Notes

Notes

Printed in the USA
CPSIA information can be obtained
at www.ICGtesting.com
LVHW010417110724
785188LV00003B/243